Bible Tales

Written by Quinlan B. Lee
Illustrated by Steve Harpster

New York   London   Toronto   Sydney

An imprint of Simon & Schuster Children's Publishing Division
1230 Avenue of the Americas, New York, New York 10020
Copyright © 2006 by Simon & Schuster, Inc.

CD copyright ℗ © MMVI Smith Management Partners
PO Box 50 Nashville, TN 37202/Martingale Music, LLC. PO Box 3711 Brentwood, TN 37024

The Bible is full of many exciting stories.

THE BIG FLOOD

A long time ago everyone had forgotten about God,
except one man named Noah.

What Could It Be?

God told Noah He was going to send a big flood.
Connect the dots to see what God told Noah to build.

Noah built an ark like God said. He brought his
family and two of every animal onto the boat.

Animal Match

Draw a line to help the animals find their matches so they can board the ark.

It rained for forty days and forty nights
until everything was covered in water.

When the sun came out, Noah sent a dove
to look for land. It didn't find anything.

Seven days later Noah sent the dove again.
It came back with an olive branch,
so Noah knew it had found dry land!

Not Like the Others

Circle the dove that is different from the others.

Noah and all the animals left the ark.

Colors of the Rainbow

What did God put in the sky to show that
He would never flood the world again?
Color by number to find out.

1-red **2-orange** **3-yellow**
4-green **5-blue** **6-purple**

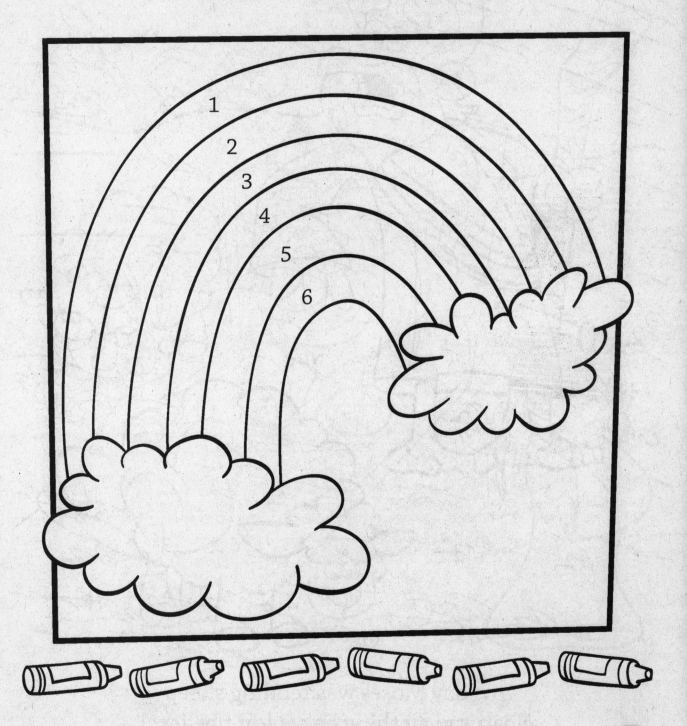

THE BURNING BUSH

One day Moses was tending sheep
and saw something he couldn't believe!

Miracle in Fire!

Color the dotted parts of the picture orange
to see what Moses saw in the desert.

When Moses got closer to the burning bush,
he heard God say, "My people are slaves in Egypt.
I am sending you to set them free."

Moses was afraid of Pharaoh, the king of Egypt.

What Could It Be?

God gave Moses an incredible sign of His power
and promised He would be with him.
*Connect the dots to see what Moses's staff became
when he threw it down.*

God also said that Aaron, Moses's brother,
would help Moses talk to Pharoah.

Moses began the long journey to Egypt.

Excursion to Egypt

Help Moses find his way through the desert to Egypt.

When Moses got to Egypt, he told Pharaoh,
"Let God's people go!"

Fancy Jewels

Pharaoh was very powerful and wore a big crown.
Color by number to see what the crown looked like.

1-blue   **2-yellow**

Pharaoh did not listen to Moses,
so God turned a river into blood.

Ribbit!

Then God made it rain frogs on Egypt.
Find and circle the ten frogs in this picture.

Next God sent gnats and flies all over the land.
The animals and the people got sick.

Feels Like a Storm

Next God sent great storms and hail.

Circle the things that you see during a storm.

When God sent locusts and darkness and death to Egypt,
Pharaoh gave up and let God's people go.

God led Moses and His people out of Egypt. They followed
a pillar of cloud by day and a pillar of fire by night.

Pharaoh's army chased God's people
through the desert.

Follow the Leader

Follow the maze to show how Pharaoh's army followed God's people.

The people were trapped between the
Red Sea and Pharaoh's army.

Secret Message

Cross out every other letter (beginning with Q) in the sentences below to see what Moses said.

DQO ENUOWTX BLEK AQFMRUATIRDE
GCOVD BWNIMLAL SFDIFGGHHT JFPOYR QYBOLU

Moses lifted his staff over the sea and said,

" _____ !

_____ !"

God made a path of dry ground
for Moses and the people.

The water crashed onto Pharaoh's army. God had set
His people free to go to His Promised Land.

THE WALLS CAME DOWN

God chose Joshua to lead His people to
the Promised Land.

Creating Words

The people were scared because the
land was filled with giants.
*Find the word that fills the blank by writing
the first letter of each picture below.*

God told the people, "Be _____ and courageous!
I have a plan to give you the land."

God told Joshua that the walls of Jericho would come down if he marched around the city.

Trumpet Time

Circle the group that has seven trumpets.

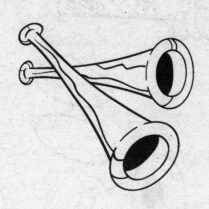

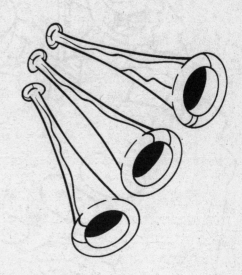

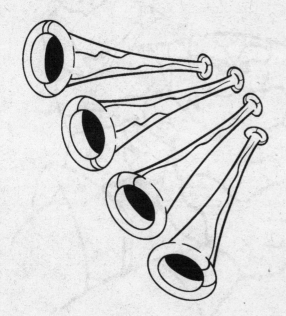

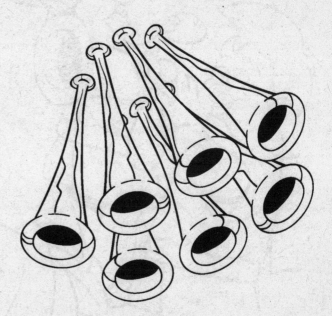

Joshua and the people obeyed God and marched once
around the city every day for six days.

Journey to Jericho

On the seventh day Joshua and the people went back to Jericho.
Help Joshua find his way through the maze to Jericho.

They marched around the city seven times, and when the trumpets blasted, the people shouted as loud as they could.

The walls came tumbling down! God had given them the city in the Promised Land.

GOD'S MIGHTY WARRIOR

God's people had to fight many battles in the
Promised Land. A farmer named Gideon led
the people to fight for God.

Even though God had chosen him, Gideon was scared.
An angel came to him and said, "Don't be afraid.
God is with you, mighty warrior!"

One Big Army

Gideon chose the biggest army he could find!
Circle the biggest group on this page.

God told Gideon to send most of the army home.
"I will win the battle," God said. "And your
army won't even have to fight."

God told Gideon to sneak into the enemy camp
with only trumpets and torches covered with jars.

Important Tools

Circle the three things God told Gideon's army to bring.

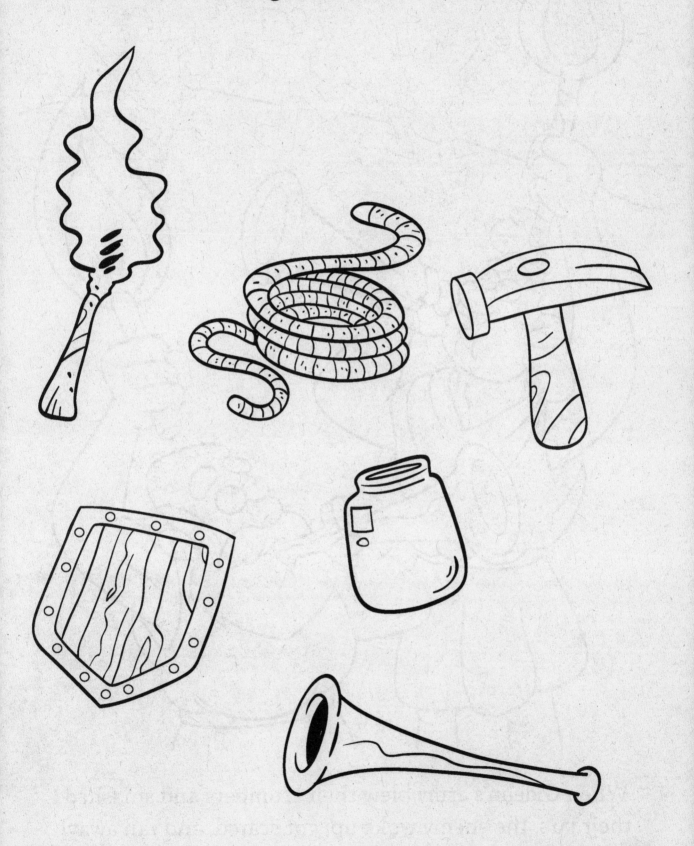

When Gideon's army blew their trumpets and smashed their jars, the enemy woke up, got scared, and ran away!

AMAZING STRENGTH

God chose a man named Samson to fight
another battle for Him.

When Samson obeyed God, he became very, very strong.
He could lift logs as big as trees and rip strong
ropes into little pieces of string.

What Could It Be?

One time Samson even wrestled a wild animal.
Connect the dots to find out which powerful animal Samson fought.

But when Samson didn't obey God, he became so weak
that his enemies were able to capture him.

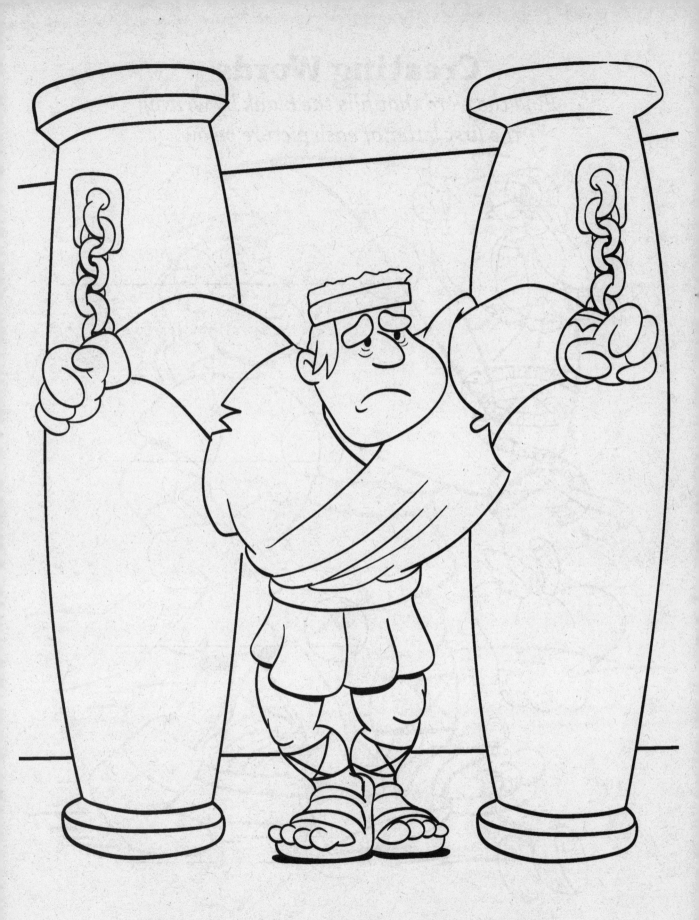

Samson's enemies tied him to two pillars.
Now who would fight for God's people?

Creating Words

Find the word that fills the blank by writing
the first letter of each picture below.

Samson didn't know what else to do,
so he began to _____.

God gave him strength to pull down the two columns
and the roof tumbled down to trap his enemies.

THE BOY AND THE GIANT

There once was a giant, Goliath,
who wanted to fight God's people.

A shepherd named David was the only person
who wasn't afraid of Goliath.

A Shepherd's Job

Do you know what animal a shepherd takes care of?

Circle it.

David knew that with God's help he could fight a giant
with a slingshot, the only weapon he owned.

Hidden Stones

David chose five smooth stones for his slingshot.
Find and circle the five stones hidden in this picture.

Goliath laughed at little David, but David was brave
and shouted, "This battle is the Lord's!"

I'm So Brave

Draw a picture of a time when you were brave.

David threw a stone, and it hit Goliath
right in the forehead.

Goliath crashed to the ground. David had
trusted God and beaten the giant.

FIRE FROM THE SKY

A king named Ahab told God's people to worship statues.
Elijah knew that people should only worship God.

Elijah organized a contest between himself
and Ahab to show the true power of God.

Matching Shapes

Draw a line to match each shape below with the
same shape somewhere in the picture.
The first one is done for you.

First Ahab and his followers prayed
and prayed. No fire came.

Elijah poured water all over his altar and
also began to pray for fire.

Not Like the Others

Which bucket is different from the others?
Circle it.

Immediately fire fell from the sky and burned the wet wood.
The people understood the true power of God.

These are just some of the amazing things that God did for His people. Look in your Bible for even more awesome stories!

Helping Hands

*Draw a picture of a time you did something
amazing for someone.*

Give Thanks

Draw a picture of something you are thankful for.

Answer Pages

Page 5:

Page 7:

Page 11:

Page 18:

Page 21:

Page 25:

Answer Pages

Page 27:

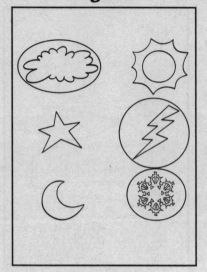

Page 37: strong

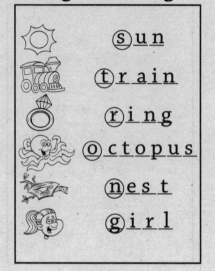

Page 31:

Page 39:

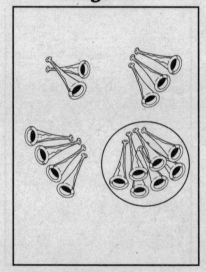

Page 33:

DO NOT BE
AFRAID!
GOD WILL
FIGHT
FOR YOU!

Page 41:

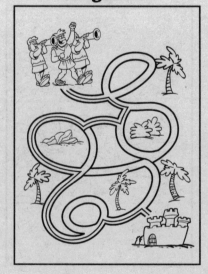

Answer Pages

Page 46:

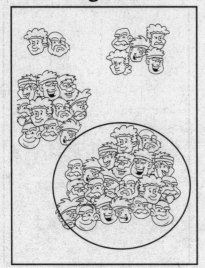

Page 56: pray

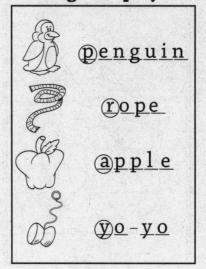

Page 49:

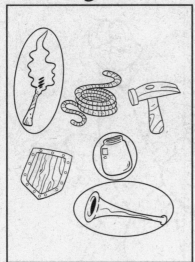

Page 60:

Page 53:

Page 62:

Answer Pages

Page 69:

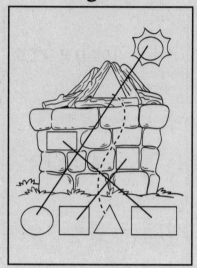

Page 72: